Written by Stephen Miller

God Loves Me

Just As I Am

For our grandchildren— and
for every child who needs to
know they are loved, seen,
and chosen just as they are.

Sometimes I wake up

feeling happy.

Sometimes I wake up

feeling sad.

Sometimes I feel

brave.

Sometimes I feel

scared.

Some days I feel big.

big.

Sometimes I feel

small.

But every day,

God sees me.

Every day,

God knows my name.

God loves me when I

laugh.

God loves me when I

cry.

God loves me when I do my best.

God loves me when I

make mistakes.

I don't have to be bigger.

I don't have to be faster.

I don't have to be different.

God loves me just
the way I am.

When I am quiet,

God is with me.

When I am loud,

God is with me.

When I feel unsure,
God holds me close.

When I feel strong,

God smiles at me.

God made me special.

God made me on purpose.

I am loved when I

play.

I am loved when I

rest.

I can talk to God anytime.

God always listens to me.

No matter what I feel...

No matter where I go...

A Bedtime Prayer

Dear God,

Thank You for loving me just as I am. Thank You for being with me today. Thank You for watching over me tonight. Help me rest, feel safe, and feel loved.

I know You are always with me.

Amen.

God loves me just as I am.

And God always will.